PHP

Troy Dimes

Contents

Your Free Gift

As a thank you for reading this book, I would like to give a gift that is a perfect companion to what you'll be learning. It's a cheat sheet that contains the most important commands that you'll need to use as well as links to detailed documentation where you can get even more help for each and every command.

To download it, visit:

http://www.linuxtrainingacademy.com/php

Thanks,

Troy

Chapter 1: Introduction & Installation

Hypertext Preprocessor, commonly known as PHP, is one of the most widely used open source, server side programming languages. Famous websites, including Facebook, Yahoo, Friendster, WordPress, and Flickr, are powered by PHP. This book provides a brief introduction to programming in PHP. In it, you'll be taught core PHP concepts, starting from the basics and moving into advanced object oriented PHP. In the first chapter of the book, you will learn how to install a development environment on your local computer in order to test the PHP pages locally before uploading them to your hosting server. Before diving into the installation details, let's look at why you should learn PHP.

Why Learn PHP?

The following are some important reasons to learn PHP as your first server side programming language.

- PHP is an open source language. This means that all PHP modules are available freely and can be customized to fit the requirements of any application.
- There are lots of free hosting services available that only support PHP; other server side languages, such as ASP.NET, have high costs associated with hosting.
- Being the first advanced server side language, PHP has a huge developer's community where you can seek help if you face issues.
- The installation and deployment of PHP based websites is a matter of few simple clicks.
- PHP supports procedural as well as object oriented programming in PHP4 and PHP5.
- PHP have several famous frameworks that can be used as the foundation for building your web applications. Some of them include WordPress, Joomla, Cake PHP, Drupal, and Symfony.

Installing the Local Server

Your PHP based web pages are going to run on a live web hosting server; however, for development and testing purposes, it is always advisable to use a local webserver. Fortunately, everything you need to install in order to run your PHP pages on local servers come packaged in a single installation known as XAMP (Operating System, Apache, MySQL and PHP). The last three characters remain constant while the operating system is a variable denoted by X. If you are using a Linux based system, you can use LAMP. Similarly, you can use a WAMP installation package for Windows-based systems. Depending on the system you have, you can download the corresponding installation package from the following link:

https://www.apachefriends.org/download.html

Note:

For this book, we are using the WAMP server. Please note that PHP script and programming syntax remains the same in different operating systems. Even if you are developing on a system other than Windows, you can follow along.

When you go to the above link, you will find options to download XAMP for different operating systems. You can choose XAMP for Windows from that page. You can download it from following link as well:

http://www.wampserver.com/en

Installation Steps:

To download and install WAMP servers on your machine, follow these steps:

1- When you click on the above link, a page will appear. The second menu item in the menu bar is the download option; click that. You will see two download options, one for 32 bit and one for 64 bit. This is shown in the following figure:

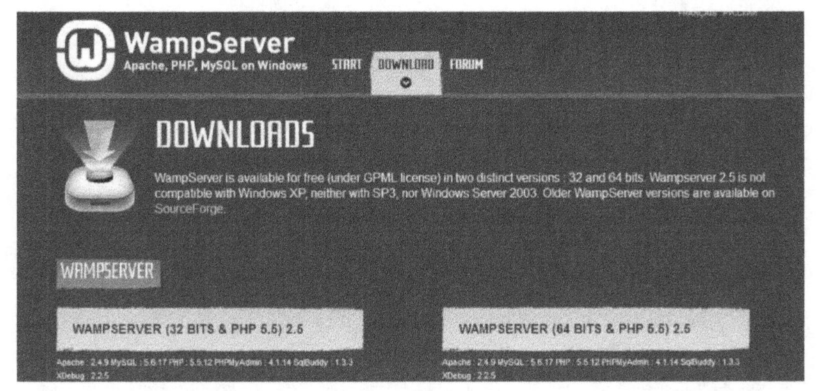

2- Once you select the OS from 32 or 64 bit, warning messages will be displayed in a pop up box. If you look at the second line, you will see the link "download directly" at the end of the second line. Click it. (Refer to figure for reference)

3- Depending on the browser (or the downloader manager) you are using, you will be presented with a download option. Download the file.

4- Now, go the directory where you downloaded the file and open it. You should see the WAMP server installation wizard. Click the "Next" button. This is shown in the following figure:

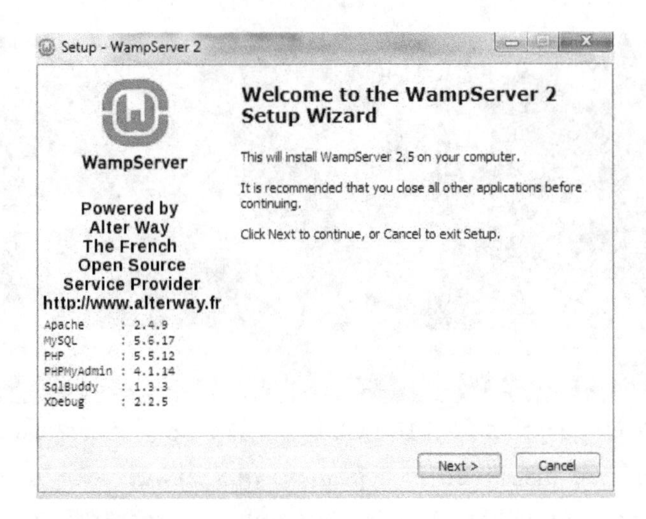

5- You will be presented with the license agreement window. Check the accept agreement radio button and click "Next". Have a look at the following figure:

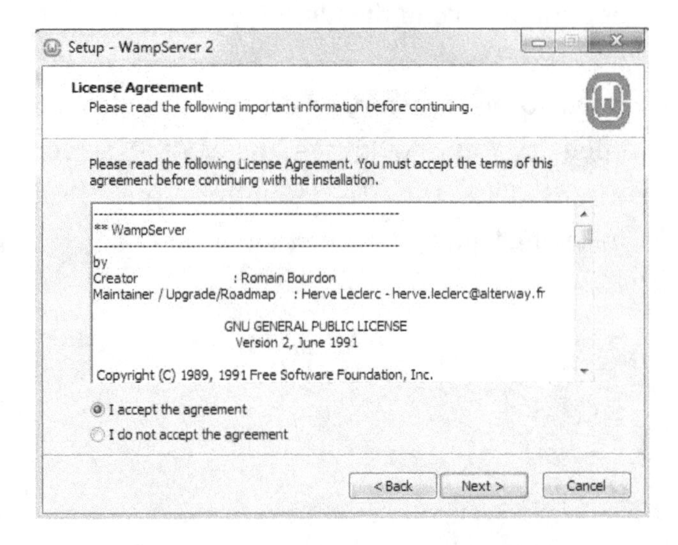

6- A new window will appear that will ask for the installation path. I recommend leaving the default path as it is and clicking the "Next" button. This is shown below:

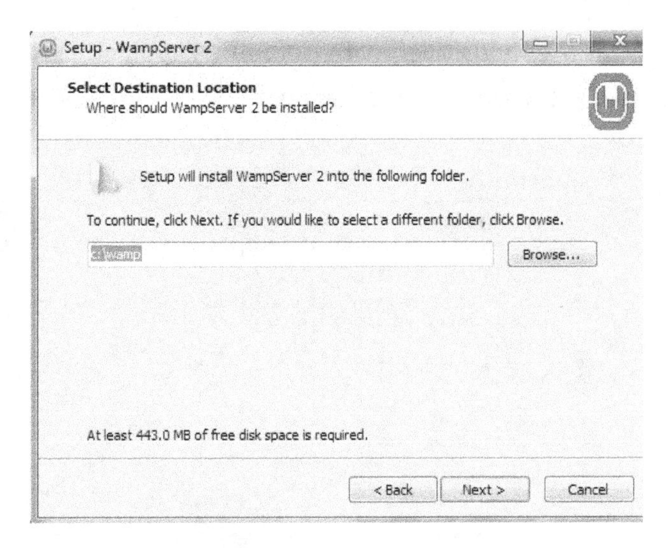

7- On the window that appears, check both boxes and click "Next". This can be seen in the following image.

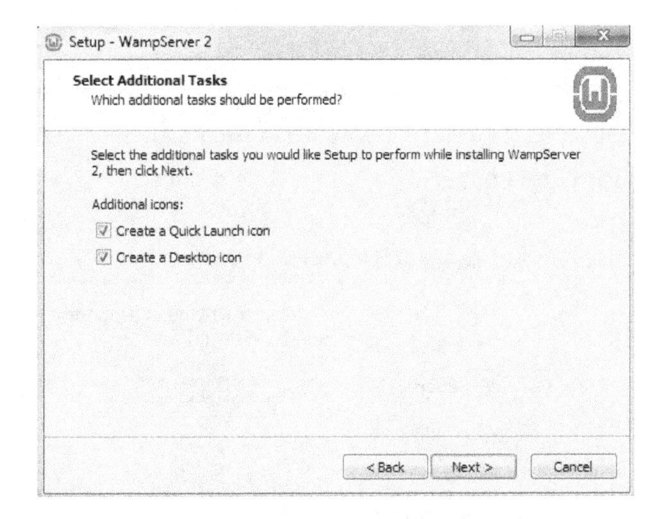

8- A dialogue box will appear. Click the "Install" button to start the installation process. During installation, the option to select the default browser will appear. Select the default browser for your web page (you can change it later). At the end of the installation, you will be presented with a window to enter the SMPT and Email servers. Leave both the fields filled with default values and click "Next". This is shown in the following figure:

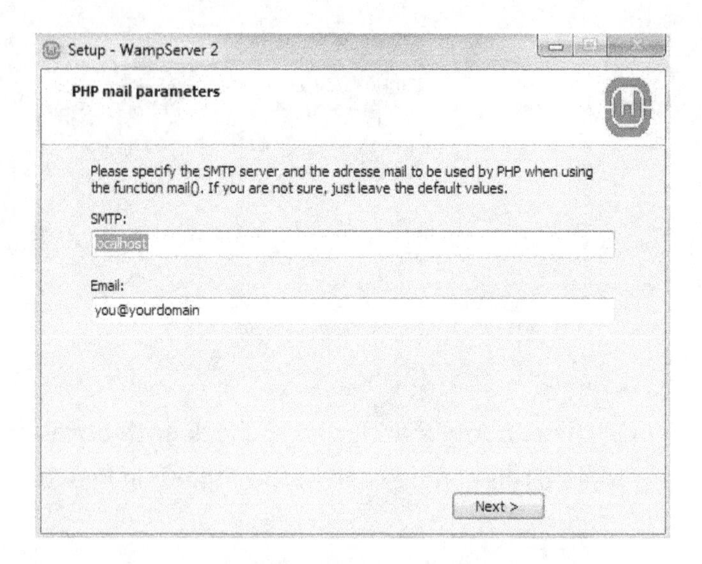

9- On the dialogue box that appears, click the "Finish" button. (Leave the only box checked). See the below figure for reference:

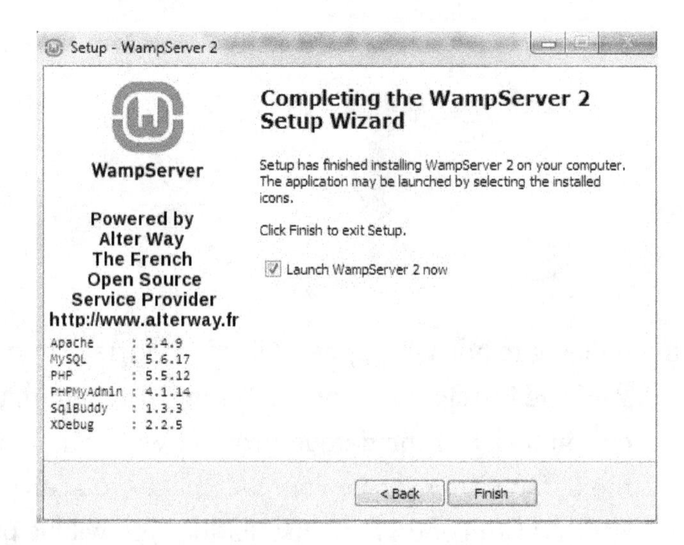

Testing the Local Server

Once you have installed the local server following the aforementioned steps, you will see a green WAMP icon at the bottom right of your system tray. This is shown in the following figure:

Click the icon. A panel should appear at the bottom right of the system, as shown in the following figure:

If you click the top option, "Localhost", you should see a webpage appear in your default browser. If your WAMP server is running successfully without any issues, you should see following page in the browser:

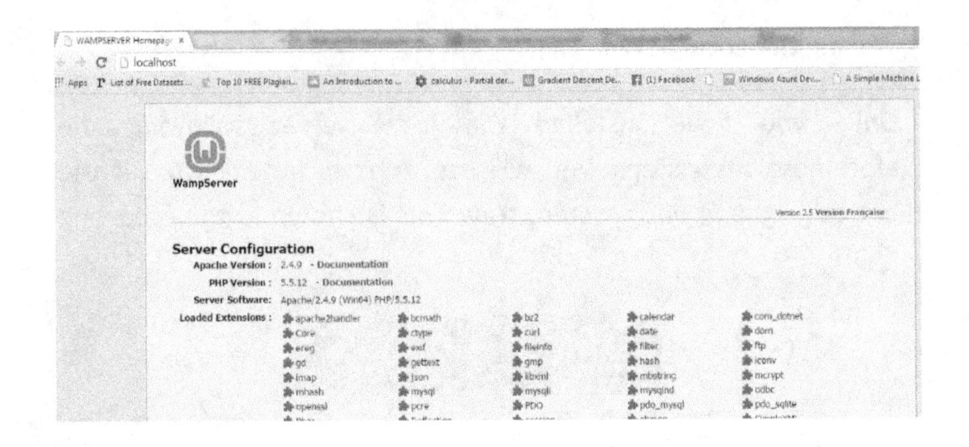

The last thing I want you to check before we end this chapter is the “www” directory. This is the directory where we will place our PHP files. In order to open this directory, again go to the WAMP panel and click the “www directory” option. This is the fourth option from the top.

Once you click the “www directory” option, your “www” directory will be opened in a new window. Your “www” directory should contain following files:

```
favicon
index.php
testmysql.php
```

And that's it for the chapter! In this chapter, we learned how to install the WAMP server. In the next chapter, we will run our first PHP program and the process of PHP parsing will be explained. Happy coding!!!

Chapter 2: PHP Basic Syntax

In the last chapter, we gave a brief introduction to PHP. We also went over how to set up the development environment. We saw how WAMP servers can be downloaded and configured, and where to place our PHP files so that the can be processed by the PHP server. In this chapter, we will learn how to write a basic program in PHP along with some other fundamental PHP concepts.

Writing your first PHP Script

In order to write your PHP script, first you need to change the file extension of your webpage to ".php". The PHP Engine parses only those files that have a ".php" extension. Now that you have your PHP page, the next step is to write the PHP code.

In a webpage, all the PHP code has to be embedded inside the opening "<?php" and closing "?>" tags. Anything outside these tags is not parsed by the PHP engine and is rendered as is by the client. For Example 1, create a webpage with any name ending with extension “.php”. Open the page in text editor and enter the following code snippet in the page.

Example 1:

```
<!DOCTYPE html>
<html>
<head>
<title>Example1</title>
</head>

<body>
<h1>This will go as it is. </h1>

<?php
echo "This is parsed by PHP";
?>

</body>
</html>
```

Place your web page in the “www” category of your WAMP server. Run your WAMP server, and enter the following URL on any browser: http://localhost/[xyz].php (Replace “xyz” with the name of your page).

You should see the following output:

This will go as it is.

This is parsed by PHP

Even though you wrote PHP code in your web page, you will find that if you right click on the webpage in your browser and click “View page source”, the page contains plain HTML, no PHP. The source for the above page in the browser will have following script.

```
<!DOCTYPE html>
<html>
<head>
<title>Example1</title>
</head>

<body>
<h1>This will go as it is. </h1>

This is parsed by PHP</body>
</html>
```

PHP Page Rendering

When the client browser sends a request to the webserver for simple HTML pages, the server immediately sends the HTML for the page to the client, which is then rendered by the webpage.

However, for PHP powered pages, the rendering mechanism is different. When a client sends a request for a page that contains PHP script, the page is first sent to the PHP engine for parsing. The PHP engine parses the script and returns the corresponding HTML, which is then sent to the client browser. This is because the client browser doesn't understand PHP; it can only understand HTML markup.

Understanding the "echo" function

In Example 1, we used the "echo" function, which is used to print plain text in a webpage. Whatever string is written after the "echo" function is parsed by the PHP engine as plain text. You can also print HTML tags via the "echo" function which will be sent as is to the client browser. In Example 2, the list of cars has been displayed in the webpage using the "echo" function.

Example 2:

```
<!DOCTYPE html>
<html>
<head>
<title>Example2</title>
</head>

<body>
<h1>Understanding PHP Echo </h1>

<?php
echo "<ul>
<li> Honda</li>
<li> Ford</li>
<li> BMW</li>
<li> Mercedez</li>
```

```
<li> Audi</li>

</ul>";

echo "<h2>The list of cars.</h2>";
?>
</body>

</html>
```

In the above example, you can see that the syntax of the unordered list has been used as the parameter for the “echo” function. When the PHP engine parses this script, it will return the string as is to the webserver, which will be rendered to client as plain HTML. In the output, an ordered list containing the names of different cars will be displayed.

It is important to note here that a PHP statement is terminated by a semicolon. In Example 2, the first “echo” statement ends with the first semicolon. The next “echo” statement simply prints an h2 heading, which contains a message. The output of the code in Example 2 will be the following webpage:

Understanding PHP Echo

- Honda
- Ford
- BMW
- Mercedez
- Audi

The list of cars.

PHP Comments

Comments are an integral part of any programming language. Comments allow programmers to write pieces of code which are not parsed by the PHP engine. Comments are there for the sake of storing information about the actual code. This information can be used by others to understand the code or to keep track of changes in the code. You can write anything you want in the comments. The syntax of commenting in PHP code is pretty straight forward.

There are two types of comments in PHP:

- Single-Line comments: These comments are used to write a comment that span one line. They start with a double forward slash, "//".
- Multi-Line comments: Multiline comments are used to write comments that span more than one line. They start with /* and end with */.

To see single-line and multi-line comments in action, have a look at the Example 3:

Example 3:

```
<!DOCTYPE html>
<html>
<head>
<title>Example3</title>
</head>

<body>
<h1>Understanding PHP Comments </h1>

<?php

/*
The following
echo statement
prints list of cars.
*/
echo "<ul>
<li>Honda</li>
<li>Ford</li>
<li>BMW</li>
<li>Mercedez</li>
<li>Audi</li>

</ul>";

// The following echo statement prints a message.
echo "<h2>The list of cars.</h2>";
?>
</body>

</html>
```

In the above code, we have added one multi-line comment above the first “echo” function, which prints the names of the cars. Next, we have added a single-line comment before the second “echo” function, which prints a simple h2 heading. If you run the above code in some browsers, the output will be similar to that of Example 2. This is because comments will be ignored by the PHP engine and no action will be taken against them.

Exercise 2

Task:

Create a PHP script which uses echo statements to display two buttons and two text boxes on separate lines. Add appropriate comments to make the code readable.

Solution:

```
<!DOCTYPE html>
<html>
<head>
<title>Exercise 2</title>
</head>

<body>
<h1>Exercise 2 Solution: </h1>

<body>
<?php
/* The following echo statement
 creates first button and text box
 */
echo '<button> Button 1 </button> <input type="text"/> <br>';
```

```
/* The following echo statement
 creates second button and text box
 */
echo '<button> Button2 </button> <input type="text"/> <br>';
?>
</body>

</html>
```

Chapter 3: Understanding Variables & String Functions

In chapter 3, we studied some of the core concepts of PHP. In this chapter, we are going to learn how variables work in PHP. We will first see how different types of variables can be declared in PHP and how they can be used. Later on, we will study some of the most commonly used PHP functions that can be used to tweak and manipulate strings in PHP. First, let's study PHP variables.

Understanding Variables in PHP

A variable is basically a place holder for values that are used at multiple places in a PHP code. For instance, when you enter your name in a login page and press enter, the name is stored in a variable and, inside the code, that variable is passed along at different places. Users do not have to enter their names again and again in order to perform different functionalities. In PHP, declaring a variable is extremely simple. You just have to prefix

"$" before the variable name. This is shown in the following example.

Example 1:

```
<!DOCTYPE html>
<html>
<head>
<title>Example 1</title>
</head>

<body>
<h1>PHP Variables</h1>

<body>
<?php

$car_name = 'Audi';
$car_price = 100;

echo $car_name;
echo '<br>';
echo $car_price;
?>
</body>

</html>
```

In Example 1, we have created two variables, car_name and car_price. The first variable stores a string while the second variable stores a number. Unlike other advanced programming languages (like C++ or Java), in PHP, the variable declaration is same for all the different types of variables. In Example 1, we have created an integer type and a string type variable via the same "$" symbol.

The PHP engine is intelligent enough to differentiate between a string and a number by looking at the quotations around the value stored in string type variable. Example 1 will have the following webpage as the output in the browser.

PHP Variables

Audi
100

Applying Operations in Variables

Different types of operations can be performed on particular variables. For instance, you can add two numeric variables as shown in Example 2.

Example 2:

```
<!DOCTYPE html>
<html>
<head>
<title>Example 2</title>
</head>

<body>
<h1>Adding two variables</h1>
```

```
<body>
<?php

$a = 5;
$b = 10;
$result = $a + $b;

echo "Result:";
echo $result;

?>
</body>

</html>
```

In the above example, we created two variables, $a and $b, and assigned them values 5 and 10, respectively. Next, we created another variable, $result, and stored the sum of $a and $b in it. Finally, we displayed the result using an echo statement. The output webpage will look like this:

Adding two variables

Result:15

Understanding Strings in PHP

Strings are formed via sequences of characters. Most of the programming languages deal with strings in the context that they contain character sequences. PHP is no different. If you look at the first example, you will see that we created a variable, $car_name, which contained a value, "Audi". Here, "Audi" is a string whereas $car_name is a string type variable. Creating a string is extremely simple in PHP. You just have to enclose a value inside single or double quotations. (I prefer single quotes).

String Functions in PHP

A function is a piece of code that performs a particular functionality and can be called again and again. Pieces of code that are required to be executed again and again can be encapsulated inside a function, which can be called later, resulting in compact code. (We shall study functions in later chapters.) In this section, we will see some of the most commonly used string functions that come built in with PHP.

- **The "." concatenation operator.**

Before studying string functions, let's see how we can concatenate two strings via a PHP "." operator. Modify Example 2 as follows:

```
<?php

$a = 5;
$b = 10;
$result = $a + $b;

echo "Result:".$result;

?>
```

Look at the "echo" function. Here we have used the dot operator to concatenate the string literal "Result:" and the $result variable. The output will be similar to that of Example 2.

- **Strlen**

The "strlen" function is used to obtain the total number of characters in a string. The "strlen" function accepts the string value as its parameters and returns the length of the string. Have a look at the following example:

```
<!DOCTYPE html>
<html>
<head>
<title>Example 3</title>
</head>

<body>
<h1>Getting length of a string</h1>

<body>

<?php
$car_name = "Audi";
echo  strlen($car_name);
$car_name = "Toyota";
echo "<br>";
echo  strlen($car_name);
?>

</body>

</html>
```

Here, we first found the length of the string, "Audi", which is 4. Then we stored Toyota in the car_name variable. If we now find the length of car_name string variable, the result will be 6, since Toyota contains 6 characters.

- **str_word_count**

This function returns the total number of words in a string. For instance, if the string is “Hello how are you?”, this function will return 4. Have a look at the following example for more details.

```
<!DOCTYPE html>
<html>
<head>
<title>String Functions</title>
</head>

<body>
<h1>Getting words in a string</h1>

<body>

<?php
$content = "Hello how are you?";
echo  str_word_count($content);
$content = "I am fine";
echo "<br>";
echo  str_word_count($content);
?>

</body>

</html>
```

In the above example, 4 will be printed on the screen followed by 3, since the string “I am fine” contains three words.

- **strrev**

The "strrev" function is used to reverse a string. Have a look at the following example.

```
<!DOCTYPE html>
<html>
<head>
<title>String Functions</title>
</head>

<body>
<h1>Reversing a string</h1>

<body>

<?php
$content = "Hello how are you?";
echo  strrev($content);
$content = "I am fine";
echo "<br>";
echo  strrev($content);
?>

</body>

</html>
```

- **Str_replace**

The "str_replace" function is used to replace contents within a string. The first parameter is the content to be replaced, the second parameter is the content which takes place of the old content, and the third parameter is the string at which you want to apply the replace function. Consider the following example.

```
<!DOCTYPE html>
<html>
<head>
<title>String Functions</title>
</head>

<body>
<h1>Replacing content within a string</h1>

<body>

<?php
$content = "Hello how are you?";
echo $content;
echo "<br>";
echo  str_replace("how", "where",$content);
?>
</body>

</html>
```

Exercise 3

Task:

Create a string type variable named “weather_info” with the value “It is cold today”. Calculate the total number of words in the string, total length of the string, and reverse the string.

Solution:

```
<!DOCTYPE html>
<html>
<head>
```

```
<title>String Functions</title>
</head>

<body>
<h1>Exercise 3 Solution</h1>

<body>

<?php
$weather_info = "It is cold today";

echo "<br>";
echo  strlen($weather_info);
echo "<br>";
echo str_word_count($weather_info);
echo "<br>";
echo strrev($weather_info);

?>

</body>

</html>
```

Chapter 4: PHP Operators

In chapter 3, we studied how variables are created and used in PHP. We also saw PHP strings and some commonly used PHP functions. In this chapter, we will briefly review different types of operators in PHP. There are five major types of operators in PHP. They are as follows:

- Arithmetic Operators
- Comparison Operators
- Assignment Operators
- Logical Operators
- Increment/Decrement Operators

1- Arithmetic Operators

Arithmetic operators in PHP are used to perform mathematical operations on numeric variables. We saw an example of addition through an arithmetic operator in the last chapter where we added two numbers. The following table contains some of the PHP arithmetic operators.

Operator	Name	Example	Output
+	Addition	$a+ $b	Sum of $a and $b
-	Subtraction	$a- $b	Difference of $a and $b
*	Multiplication	$a* $b	Product of $a and $b
/	Division	$a/ $b	Quotient of $a and $b
%	Modulus	$a% $b	Remainder of $a divided by $b
**	Exponentiation	$a** $b	Result of raising $ a to the $b'th power

In Example 1 of this chapter, we will see some arithmetic operations in action.

Example 1:

```
<!DOCTYPE html>
<html>
<head>
<title>Chapter 4</title>
</head>

<body>
<h1>Arithmetic Operators</h1>

<body>
```

```
<?php
$a = 50;
$b = 10;

echo $a + $b;
echo "<br>";
echo $a - $b;
echo "<br>";
echo $a * $b;
echo "<br>";
echo $a / $b;

?>

</body>

</html>
```

In the above example, we have created two variables, $a and $b, with values 50 and 10 respectively. We have then applied addition, subtraction, multiplication, and division operations on these variables. The output of the above code will be a webpage containing this data:

Arithmetic Operators

60
40
500
5

2- Comparison Operators

In PHP, comparison operators are used for comparing the values of numbers and strings. The following table contains information about commonly used comparison operators.

Operator	Name	Example	Output
==	Equal	$a == $b	Returns true if $a is equal to $b
===	Identical	$a === $b	Returns true if $a is equal to $b, and they are of the same type
!=	Not equal	$a != $b	Returns true if $a is not equal to $b
<>	Not equal	$a <> $b	Returns true if $a is not equal to $b
!==	Not identical	$a !== $b	Returns true if $a is not equal to $b, or they are not of the same type
>	Greater than	$a > $b	Returns true if $a is greater than $b
<	Less than	$a < $b	Returns true if $a is less than $b
>=	Greater than or equal to	$a >= $b	Returns true if $a is greater than or equal to $b

<=	Less than or equal to	$a <= $b	Returns true if $a is less than or equal to $b

These operators will be used in future chapters, where we will be studying control statements such as “if” and “else”.

3- Assignment Operators

Assignment operators are used to assign values from one operator to another. The following table contains some of the most commonly used assignment operators.

Assignment	Similar to	What it does
a = b	a = b	The left operand is set to the value of the operand on the right
a += b	a = a + b	Addition
a -= b	a = a - b	Subtraction
a *= b	a = a * b	Multiplication
a /= b	a = a / b	Division
a %= b	a = a % b	Modulus

Have a look at Example 2 to see assignment operators in action.

Example 2:

```
<!DOCTYPE html>
<html>
<head>
<title>Chapter 4</title>
</head>

<body>
<h1>Assignment Operators</h1>

<body>

<?php
$a = 50;
$b = 10;

$a += $b;

echo $a;
echo"<br>";
$a = 50;

$a -= $b;

echo $a;
echo"<br>";
$a = 50;

$a *= $b;

echo $a;
echo"<br>";
$a = 50;

$a /= $b;
```

```
echo $a;
echo"<br>";
$a = 50;

$a %= $b;

echo $a;

?>

</body>

</html>
```

4- Logical Operators

In PHP, logical operators are used to perform real world logic operations, such as AND, OR, NOT, and NAND. Logical operators are applied on operands of Boolean types. The following table contains information about commonly used logical operators in PHP.

Operator	Name	Example	Output
and	And	$a and $b	True if both $a and $b are true
or	Or	$a or $b	True if either $a or $b is true
xor	Xor	$a xor $b	True if either $a or $b is true, but not both

<table>
<tr><td>&&</td><td>And</td><td>$a && $b</td><td>True if both $a and $b are true</td></tr>
<tr><td>||</td><td>Or</td><td>$a || $b</td><td>True if either $a or $b is true</td></tr>
<tr><td>!</td><td>Not</td><td>!$a</td><td>True if $a is not true</td></tr>
</table>

We shall see logical operators in action in future chapters.

5- Increment/Decrement Operators

These variables are used to increase or decrease the value of numeric variables by one. The following table contains PHP increment and decrement operators.

Operator	Name	What it does
++$a	Pre-increment	Increments $a by one, then returns $a
$a++	Post-increment	Returns $a, then increments $a by one
--$a	Pre-decrement	Decrements $a by one, then returns $a
$a--	Post-decrement	Returns $a, then decrements $a by one

See Example 3 for examples of increment and decrement operators in action.

Example 3:

```
<!DOCTYPE html>
<html>
<head>
<title>Chapter 4</title>
</head>

<body>
<h1>Increment & Decrement Operators</h1>

<body>

<?php
$a = 45;
echo ++$a;
echo "<br>";
echo $a++;
echo "<br>";
echo --$a;
echo "<br>";
echo $a--;
?>

</body>

</html>
```

In the above example, variable $a has been initialized with a value of 45. We have then applied the pre-increment operator to it and displayed its value, which will become 46. Next, we again displayed its value, then applied post-increment to it. The displayed value will be 46 but the actual value will be 47 now.

Next, we pre-decremented the value and then echoed it; this time, again, 46 will be displayed. Finally we again displayed the value and then post-decremented it, which means that displayed value will again be 46 but actually $a contains 45 at the moment. In the output, 46 will be displayed 4 times.

Exercise 4

Task:

Create two variables, $number1 and $number2, and assign them the values 36 and 6, respectively. Apply the four basic arithmetic operations between these variables and output the result on a webpage.

Solution

```
<!DOCTYPE html>
<html>
<head>
<title>Chapter 4</title>
</head>

<body>
<h1>Exercise 4 Solution.</h1>

<body>

<?php
$number1 = 36;
$number2 = 6;

echo $number1 + $number2;
echo "<br>";
echo $number1 - $number2;
```

```
echo "<br>";
echo $number1 * $number2;
echo "<br>";
echo $number1 / $number2;

?>


</body>

</html>
```

Chapter 5: Iteration and Control Statements

In the previous chapters, we have studied variables and operators. Now we will begin studying iteration statements and control statements, which are two of the core programming concepts in PHP. Iteration statements in PHP help iteratively execute a particular piece of code for a desired number of times. Control statements are used to control application execution path. In this chapter, we are going to review both of these concepts with the help of examples.

1- Iteration Statements

At times, you may want to execute same piece of code multiple times. You can either write the code itself the number of times you want to execute it, or you can use iteration statements, which are faster and more robust. There are two major types of iteration statements in PHP.

- **The "for" loop**

The “for” loop is the most commonly used iteration statement. A “for” loop executes a piece of code an exact number of times. It doesn’t require any termination flag to terminate its execution. You simply specify the number of iterations in the loop declaration, and the loop will execute the corresponding number of times. The “for” loop should be used when you know the exact number of iterations in advance. Take a look at the first example, where we are going to print the table of 10 using a “for” loop.

Example 1:

```
<!DOCTYPE html>
<html>
<head>
<title>Chapter 5</title>
</head>

<body>
<h1>The for loop.</h1>

<body>

<?php

for($k=1; $k<=10; $k++)
{
        $output = 10*$k;
        echo "<li> 10 x".$k." = ".$output."</li>";
}
?>

</body>

</html>
```

The above piece of code will print the table of 10 on the output webpage. Have a look at the “for” loop in the above code:

```
for($k=1; $k<=10; $k++)
{
        $output = 10*$k;
        echo "<li> 10 x".$k." = ".$output."</li>";
}
```

The “for” loop declaration has three parts: initialization counter, test counter, and increment counter. In Example 1, $k=1 is the initialization counter, which means that loop will start with $k=1. The $k<=10 is the test counter, which states that loop will keep executing until $k<=10. Lastly is the increment counter, which is incremented with every loop execution. The number of iterations of a loop is decided by these three counters. The output of Example 1 is as follows:

The for loop.

10 x1 = 10
10 x2 = 20
10 x3 = 30
10 x4 = 40
10 x5 = 50
10 x6 = 60
10 x7 = 70
10 x8 = 80
10 x9 = 90
10 x10 = 100

- **The “while” loop**

The “while” loop keeps executing until a certain condition is met. For instance, if you want to keep executing a piece of code until a value is less than 10, you can use a “while” loop. In Example 2, we will show you how you can print a table of 10 using a “while” loop.

Example 2:

```
<!DOCTYPE html>
<html>
<head>
<title>Chapter 5</title>
</head>

<body>
<h1>The while loop.</h1>

<?php
$k=1;
while($k<=10)
{
        $output = 10*$k;
        echo "<li> 10 x".$k." = ".$output."</li>";
        $k++;
}
?>

</body>

</html>
```

You can see in the “while” loop declaration that it only takes one parameter. This is basically the termination flag or condition. The "while" loop keeps executing until this condition returns true. As soon as the condition returns false, the "while" loop stops executing.

2- Control Statements

As explained earlier, control statements are used to control the flow of the application. Consider the example of a shopping cart website. A user selects a product, clicks on the "add to cart" option, and selects a country where the product has to be shipped. If there are shipping services in the selected country, the selection will be processed; otherwise the selection is not processed and a message appears that shipping services not available for your country. This processing logic is powered by control statements. There are two types of control statements in PHP.

- **If/else statement**

Let's jump straight into a working example to see how if/else statements work.

Example 3:

```
<!DOCTYPE html>
<html>
<head>
<title>Chapter 5</title>
</head>

<body>
<h1>if/else loop.</h1>

<body>
```

```
<?php

$country = "uvw";

if($country =="abc" || $country == "xyz")
{
        echo "<h2>Shipping Services Not
Available</h2>";
}
else if ($country=="uvw")
{
        echo '<h2>Shipping takes 10 days. Are you
willing to proceed?</h2>';
}
else
{
        echo "<h2> Your order has been placed.</h2>";
}
?>

</body>

</html>
```

In the above code, we have created a variable, $country, and have assigned it a random name, “uvw”. Using an if statement, we checked if the name of the country is equal to “abc” or “xyz”. If this condition returns true, the message will be printed that no shipping services are available for the chosen country and the remaining conditions will not be checked. However, since the variable $country neither contains “abc“ nor “xyz”, the first condition will return false and the second if/else condition will be checked. The second condition will return true; since the $country variable contains “uvw”, the message inside the second if/else block will be printed. If none of the if and if/else statements return true, the code in the last else statement executes. The output of Example 3 will be as follows:

if/else loop.

Shipping takes 10 days. Are you willing to proceed?

- **The switch statement**

If you have to make a decision based on large number of conditions, it is not recommended to use multiple if/else blocks. In such scenarios, using a switch statement is a better option. Have a look at Example 4 to see how switch statements work in PHP.

Example 4:

```
<!DOCTYPE html>
<html>
<head>
<title>Chapter 5</title>
</head>

<body>
<h1>Switch Statements.</h1>

<body>

<?php

$country = "uvw";

switch ($country)
{
```

```
case "abc":
echo '<h2>Shipping Services Not Available</h2>';
break;

case "xyz":
echo '<h2>Shipping Services Not Available</h2>';
break;

case "uvw":
echo '<h2>Shipping takes 10 days. Are you willing to
proceed?</h2>';
break;

default:
echo '<h2> Your order has been placed.</h2>';
break;
}

?>

</body>

</html>
```

In Example 4, we have used a switch statement to implement the shipping scenario that we implemented in Example 3. The output of Example 4 is as follows:

Switch Statements.

Shipping takes 10 days. Are you willing to proceed?

Exercise 5

Task:

Display the factorial of 7 using a “while” loop.

Solution

```
<!DOCTYPE html>
<html>
<head>
<title>Exercise 5</title>
</head>

<body>
<h1>Exercise 5 Solution.</h1>

<body>

<?php

$output = 1;
$input=7;
$k=1;
while( $k<=$input)
{
        $output = $k * $output;
        $k++;
}
echo $output;

?>
```

```
</body>

</html>
```

Chapter 6: Understanding PHP Arrays

Arrays are used to store collections of data in contiguous memory locations. Arrays are handy in scenarios where you have to store a collection of data, such as the names of all students in a school or the prices of cars. In such scenarios, creating a variable for each value is cumbersome. Using arrays is the right option in such cases. In this chapter, we will learn what different types of arrays are, how they can be created, and how to add and retrieve elements from the arrays.

Creating Arrays in PHP

The process of creating arrays in PHP is very similar to creating variables. You simply have to write $ followed by the name of the array and opening and closing square brackets. This brings up a question regarding the usage of square brackets. The answer is simple; in the case of variables, you are storing a single value; in the case of arrays, you are storing a collection of items. Therefore, the position, or index, where the items are going to be stored is specified in the square brackets. Note than an array in PHP has zero based indexing. This means that the first element is at the zero index and the last element is stored at the n-1st index, where 'n' is the total number of elements.

It's time to jump into our first working example. We will create a "countries" array which will store the names of countries:

Example 1:

```
<!DOCTYPE html>
<html>
<head>
<title>Chapter 6</title>
</head>

<body>
<h1>Arrays in PHP</h1>

<body>

<?php

$countries[0]= "USA";
$countries[1]= "RUSSIA";
$countries[2]= "CANADA";
$countries[3]= "CHINA";
$countries[4]= "ENGLAND";

$countries[]= "FRANCE";
$countries[]= "ITALY";
$countries[]= "GERMANY";
$countries[]= "SPAIN";
$countries[]= "PORTUGAL";
```

```
print_r($countries);

?>

</body>

</html>
```

In Example 1, we created an array named “countries” and stored the names of some random countries in it. If you closely look at the countries array, we have specified the index for the first five items. For the 6th to 10th items, starting from “FRANCE”, we did not specify the element. The PHP engine is intelligent enough to assign this item the next available index, which is 6th. There are two ways in which we can insert elements into a PHP array. We can either specify the index ourselves or let the PHP engine find the next available index and store the elements. Finally, we used the print_r method to print the contents of the array. The output page for Example 1 will contain following content:

```
Arrays in PHP

Array ( [0] => USA [1] => RUSSIA [2] => CANADA [3] => CHINA [4] => ENGLAND [5] => FRANCE [6] => ITALY [7] => GERMANY [8] => SPAIN [9] => PORTUGAL )
```

Creating Arrays using an “Array” Keyword

In addition to creating arrays using an index based approach, you can also create arrays using the “array” keyword. This is an advanced approach. Using this approach, you can store elements in an array during declaration. In Example 2, we will store items in the country array using the “array” keyword.

Example 2:

```
<!DOCTYPE html>
<html>
<head>
<title>Chapter 6</title>
</head>

<body>
<h1>Using Array Keyword and Foreach</h1>

<body>

<?php

$countries = array('USA', 'CANADA', 'CHINA',
'FRANCE', 'ENGLAND');

foreach($countries as $country)
{
        echo $country."<br>";
}

?>

</body>

</html>
```

In Example 2, there are a couple of important concepts to comprehend. First is the usage of the "array" keyword. The second is the "foreach" loop. Here, the "foreach" loop is use to iterate over the array. "Foreach" loops are better than "for" loops when you have to iterate a collection of items, since you don't have to specify the number of times you want to execute the loop. PHP engine is intelligent enough to find the number of items and execute the "foreach" loop corresponding number of times. If you're still wondering how to traverse an array using a "for" loop, have a look at the next section.

Array Traversal using "For" Loops.

Example 3 demonstrates how to use "for" loops for array traversal.

Example 3:

```
<!DOCTYPE html>
<html>
<head>
<title>Chapter 6</title>
</head>

<body>
<h1>Array Traversal</h1>

<body>

<?php

$countries[0]= "USA";
$countries[1]= "RUSSIA";
$countries[2]= "CANADA";
$countries[3]= "CHINA";
$countries[4]= "ENGLAND";

$countries[]= "FRANCE";
$countries[]= "ITALY";
$countries[]= "GERMANY";
```

```
$countries[]= "SPAIN";
$countries[]= "PORTUGAL";


echo '<ul>';
for($x=0;$x<10;$x++)
{
        echo '<li>'.$countries[$x].'</li>';
}
echo '</ul>';

?>


</body>

</html>
```

You can see in the above example that you can use a “for” loop to iterate through the items in the countries array and display them in the form of an unordered list. The output page of Example 3 will contain an unordered list as displayed below:

Array Traversal

- USA
- RUSSIA
- CANADA
- CHINA
- ENGLAND
- FRANCE
- ITALY
- GERMANY
- SPAIN
- PORTUGAL

Associative Arrays

An associative array is a type of array where you specify the name of the index at which the element is going to be stored, rather than a numeric index. Associative arrays are more readable since index numbers don't convey any concrete message. On the other hand, a text-based index is not only easy to remember, but can also store some info about the item. Have a look at Example 4 to see how associative arrays work.

Example 4:

```
<!DOCTYPE html>
<html>
<head>
<title>Chapter 6</title>
</head>

<body>
```

```
<h1>Associative Array</h1>

<body>

<?php

$countries['America1']= "USA";
$countries['Europe1']= "RUSSIA";
$countries['America2']= "CANADA";
$countries['Asia1']= "CHINA";
$countries['Europe2']= "ENGLAND";

echo $countries['Asia1'].'<br>';
echo $countries['Europe1'].'<br>';

?>


</body>

</html>
```

In Example 4, we again created a countries array; however, this time instead of passing it the index number, we passed a text-based index. For instance, the index for the item "USA" is "America1" and for "CHINA" is "Asia1". Similarly, we can use this text based index to access the items. We have done this by retrieving elements at indexes "Asia1" and "Europe1". The output page for the above example will contain following content:

Associative Array

CHINA
RUSSIA

Exercise 6

Task:

Create a random array of 10 integers. Find the largest and smallest numbered integer in an array using a loop. Display the result using echo.

Solution:

```
<!DOCTYPE html>
<html>
<head>
<title>Exercise 6</title>
</head>

<body>
<h1>Exercise 6 Solution</h1>

<body>

<?php

$integers = array(48,15,45,65,26,78,19,35,64,76);

$largest=0;
$smallest = 0;

foreach($integers as $integer)
```

```
{
        if($integer > $largest)
        {
                $largest = $integer;
        }

        if($smallest == 0)
        {
                $smallest = $integer;
        }
        else if($integer < $smallest)
        {
                $smallest = $integer;
        }
}

echo $largest.'<br>';
echo $smallest;

?>


</body>

</html>
```

Chapter 7: Functions in PHP

A function is a piece of code that encapsulates a particular functionality and can be called whenever that functionality is needed. Suppose you have three integer type arrays and you are assigned the task of finding the largest and smallest elements of each array. One approach is to write the logic of finding the largest and smallest elements three times, one for each array. The other approach is to encapsulate the logic inside a function and, whenever you want to find the largest and smallest item in the array, you can call this function. The latter approach is not only compact but also results in organized and standard code.

In this chapter, we will learn how to create functions, how to pass values to a function, and how a function can return a value to the calling function. First we will look at how a function can be created in PHP and how it is called.

Example 1:

```
<!DOCTYPE html>
<html>
<head>
<title>Chapter 7</title>
</head>

<body>

<?php

function displayTagLine()
{
        echo "<h1>A Place for Top Cars </h1>";
}

displayTagLine();
 echo "<p> We sell new and used cars at a price much
lower than our competitors. <br>
 You can also rent new and used cars with or without
a driver.</p>";

displayTagLine();

?>

</body>

</html>
```

In Example 1, we created a function called displayTagLine() which prints a message in the h1 header. The syntax of creating a function is very straight forward. You have to start with the keyword function, followed by the name of the function, and, lastly, opening and closing round brackets. Inside the round brackets, the parameters accepted by the function are mentioned. The function body starts with an opening curly bracket and ends with a closing curly bracket. Inside these brackets, insert the code that you want to execute whenever you call the function.

To call a function, write the function name and pass the parameter to the function (if any) inside the round brackets. Since, the function displayTagLine() does not accept any parameters, we call left the round brackets empty. In the next section, we will see how we can pass parameters to the function.

Parameterized Functions

To write parameterized functions, you have to specify them in the opening and closing brackets; when you call the function, you have to pass the corresponding values to the function call. Let us modify Example 1 so that the displayTagLine() function will accept a message that will be displayed by the function. Have a look at Example 2.

Example 2:

```
<!DOCTYPE html>
<html>
<head>
<title>Chapter 7</title>
</head>

<body>

<?php

function displayTagLine($message)
{
        echo '<h2>'.$message.'</h2>';
```

```
}

displayTagLine('We sell best quality cars.');
 echo "<p> We sell new and used cars at a price much
lower than our competitors. <br>
 You can also rent new and used cars with or without
a driver.</p>";

displayTagLine('Comfortable cars for rent.');

?>

</body>

</html>
```

In Example 2, the displayTagLine() function accepts one parameter; inside the function, the value of that parameter is printed. If you look at the calls to this function, a string value has been passed to the function. You can call the displayTagLine() method as many times as you want to display different tag lines. The output of the code in Example 2 is as follows:

We sell best quality cars.

We sell new and used cars at a price much lower than our competitors.
You can also rent new and used cars with or without a driver.

Comfortable cars for rent.

Returning Values from Functions

In addition to passing values to functions via parameters, you can also get the values from a function using the “return” keyword. In

Example 3, we will pass two parameters to a function, take the square of both, and return the sum.

Example 3:

```
<!DOCTYPE html>
<html>
<head>
<title>Chapter 7</title>
</head>

<body>

<?php

function sumOfSquares($num1, $num2)
{
        return ($num1* $num1) + ($num2 * $num2);
}
echo sumOfSquares(2,3);

?>

</body>

</html>
```

In Example 3, we have created a function named sumOfSquares. This function accepts two variables. Inside the function, we squared the variables and took their sum. The result has been returned using the "return" keyword. This result has been printed using the "echo" function. In the output, you will see 13, which is ((2x2) + (3x3)).

Passing Values to Functions by Reference

In Example 2 and Example 3 of this chapter, we passed parameters to the function. Those parameters were passed by value, which means that, inside the function, the copy of the passed value is created and all the processing is done on that copy. The actually passed value is not disturbed. On the other hand, when parameters are passed by reference, the actual value is not passed but the reference of the value is passed. If the value is changed inside the function, the change is also reflected in the calling function. In Example 4, we will see how parameters can be passed by references.

Example 4:

```
<!DOCTYPE html>
<html>
<head>
<title>Chapter 7</title>
</head>

<body>

<?php

$num1=10;
$num2 = 5;

echo 'Before Passing by reference:'.$num1.'-
'.$num2.'<br>';
SquareByRef($num1, $num2);
echo 'After Passing by reference:'.$num1.'-'.$num2;

function SquareByRef(&$a, &$b)
{
        $a= $a * $a;
        $b = $b * $b;
```

```
}

?>

</body>

</html>
```

In Example 4, we created a function called SquareByRef which takes two reference type parameters. You can see that in order to pass a variable by reference, you simply have to append the ampersand sign before the parameter. We created two variables, $num1 and $num2, and passed them by reference to the SquareByRef function. Inside the function, we squared both of them and returned nothing. Next, we displayed the $num1 and $num2 variables both before and after calling the function. In the output, you will see that the values will be different because the SquareByRef method will change the actual values that were passed by reference. The output of Example 4 will be a webpage containing this content.

```
Before Passing by reference:10-5
After Passing by reference:100-25
```

Exercise 7

Task:

Create three integer type arrays. Create a function which displays the largest and smallest elements of these arrays. Display the output on screen.

Solution

```
<!DOCTYPE html>
<html>
<head>
<title>Exercise 7</title>
</head>

<body>

<?php

$integers = array(48,15,45,65,26,78,19,35,64,76);
$integers2 = array(41,25,65,47,89,12,35,4,76,98);
$integers3 = array(12,36,47,58,96,32,56,41,59,74);


processArray($integers);
processArray($integers2);
processArray($integers3);

function processArray($array)
{
$largest=0;
$smallest = 0;

foreach($array as $item)
{
        if($item > $largest)
        {
                $largest = $item;
        }
```

```
        if($smallest == 0)
        {
                $smallest = $item;
        }
        else if($item < $smallest)
        {
                $smallest = $item;
        }
}

echo '<br><br>';
echo $largest.'<br>';
echo $smallest.'<br>';

}

?>

</body>

</html>
```

Chapter 8: Object Oriented PHP (Part 1)

In the earliest days of programming, the primary coding approach was procedural or structural programming where the code was used to execute a sequence. However, that approach lacked modularity and reusability. To address these issues, the object oriented programming approach was introduced. OOP encapsulates real world scenarios by packaging real world entities into objects that have certain characteristics and can perform a certain function. Initially, languages like C++ and JAVA adopted the OOP paradigm; however, with the passage of time, other languages also began to embrace this revolutionary idea. PHP is one of them.

In this chapter, we will learn how to create a class in PHP and how to add functions and member variables to it.

PHP Class

As aforementioned, a class maps out a real world entity. Anything having some characteristics and performing some functions can be packaged as a class. Consider the example of a blog. It has a user who can create posts; a post can belong to a category and can contain an image or a video. In this scenario, there are several entities that can be encapsulated inside a class. We can have a User class, a Post class, a Category class, and so on. In Example 1, we will show you how to create a class in PHP. We shall create a User class.

Example 1:

```
<!DOCTYPE html>
<html>
<head>
<title>Chapter 8</title>
</head>

<body>

<?php

class  User{
    /* Member variables */
    var $name;
        var $email;
    var $password;

    /* Member functions */
    function signUp($uname, $upassword, $uemail){

           $this->name = $uname;
           $this->password = $upassword;
           $this->email = $uemail;
    }
```

```
        function getName()
        {
        return $this->name;
        }
}
?>


</body>

</html>
```

To create a class in PHP, you have to use the keyword "class" followed by the class name and opening and closing curly brackets. Inside these brackets, the member variables and functions of the class are encapsulated. In Example 1, we created a class, User. This class contains three member variables: $name, $email, and $password. The class contains two methods, signUp and getName.

The first method takes three parameters that are used to initialize the three member variables of the class. To access member variables within a class, you can use the "$this" keyword which refers to the current object. Using the "$this" keyword, we assigned values passed in the parameter of the signUp function to the class member variables. The getName method simply returns the $name variable to the calling function.

Object (Place holder for a class)

A class itself is nothing but a blue print. The concept of classes and objects can be compared to the context of a blueprint of a house. A class is like a map, in that it has no physical existence, and it is just a template which can be used for building a house. Objects, on the other hand, have actual physical existence. As multiple houses can be constructed on the basis of single map, a class can also have multiple objects. In Example 2, we will see how to create an object of a class and how we can use a call function to access member variables of a class via its object.

Example 2:

```
<!DOCTYPE html>
<html>
<head>
<title>Chapter 8</title>
</head>

<body>

<?php

class  User{
    /* Member variables */
    var $name;
        var $email;
    var $password;

    /* Member functions */
    function signUp($uname, $upassword, $uemail){

           $this->name = $uname;
           $this->password = $upassword;
           $this->email = $uemail;
    }

        function getName()
        {
        return $this->name;
```

```
        }
}

$user1 = new User;
$user2 = new User;

$user1->signUp("Jack", "12345", "abc@xyz.com");

$user2->signUp("Mark", "879789", "abcd@xyz1.com");

echo $user1->getName().'<br>';
echo $user1->email.'<br>';
echo $user2->getName().'<br>';
?>


</body>

</html>
```

In Example 2, we created two objects in the User class. Have a look at the end of the User class. To create the object in a class, the new keyword is used. This keyword creates a new object in a class and returns the reference of the object. In Example 2, we have two variables, user1 and user2, that store references of the User class objects. Next, we have called the signUp function on both objects and have passed three random parameters to this function.

To call a function via object, you have to write the name of the object followed by "->" and the function name. Accessing member variables is similar. We have accessed the email member variable of the user1 object. Finally, we displayed the name of both objects via echo by calling the getName functions on user1 and user2. The output of Example 2 is as follows:

```
Jack
abc@xyz.com
Mark
```

Using a Constructor for Member Initialization

In OOP, a constructor is a method that is used to initialize the member variables. Whenever you create an object using the “new” keyword, this constructor function is called, thereby initializing the member variables. In most programming languages, a constructor is a function with the same name as the class name. However, in PHP, a __construct() function is used as constructor. Example 3 shows a PHP constructor in action.

Example 3:

```
<!DOCTYPE html>
<html>
<head>
<title>Chapter 8</title>
</head>

<body>

<?php

class  User{
    /* Member variables */
    var $name;
        var $email;
```

```
    var $password;

    /* Member functions */
    function __construct($uname, $upassword,
$uemail){

            $this->name = $uname;
            $this->password = $upassword;
            $this->email = $uemail;
    }

        function getName()
        {
        return $this->name;
        }
}

$user1 = new User("Jack", "12345", "abc@xyz.com");
$user2 = new User("Mark", "879789", "abcd@xyz1.com");

echo $user1->getName().'<br>';
echo $user1->email.'<br>';
echo $user2->getName().'<br>';
?>


</body>

</html>
```

In the above code, we replaced the signUp method with the constructor function. In order to initialize the member variables we don't have to call the signup method. Rather, at the time of creation of an object, we shall utilize the constructor and pass the parameter to it. For instance, look at the following line of code:

```
$user1 = new User("Jack", "12345", "abc@xyz.com");
```

Here we have created an object of User class using the new keyword. In addition, we passed three parameters in the opening and closing round brackets. This is the call to the constructor that takes three parameters. Next, we have again called the getName method to see if member variables have been initialzed or not. The output of Example 3 shall be similar to that of Example 2.

Exercises 8

Task:

Create a class named Item with three member variables: $name, $price, and $category. Use a constructor to initialize these member variables. Add a method which returns the name of the category of item. Create two objects in the Item class and display the category.

Solution:

```
<!DOCTYPE html>
<html>
<head>
<title>Chapter 8</title>
</head>

<body>

<?php
```

```
class  Item{
    /* Member variables */
    var $name;
        var $price;
    var $category;

    /* Member functions */
    function __construct($iname, $iprice,
$icategory){

            $this->name = $iname;
            $this->price = $iprice;
            $this->category = $icategory;
    }

        function getCategory()
        {
        return $this->category;
        }
}

$item1 = new Item("TV", "400", "Electronics");
$item2 = new Item("Table", "200", "Furniture");

echo $item1->getCategory().'<br>';
echo $item2->getCategory().'<br>';
?>


</body>

</html>
```

Chapter 9: Object Oriented PHP (Part 2)

In chapter 8, we studied how classes and objects can be created and how constructor functions can be used to initialize member variables. In this chapter, we will further explore some of the other important OOP concepts in PHP, starting with inheritance.

Inheritance

Inheritance refers to the ability of a class to inherit properties from another class. A class which inherits another class is called the "derived" class or the "child" class, while the class that is inherited by other classes is called the "parent" class or "base" class. When a class inherits another class, it inherits the member variables as well as member functions of that class.

Example 1:

```
<!DOCTYPE html>
```

```
<html>
<head>
<title>Chapter 9</title>
</head>

<body>

<?php

class Item
{
        var $name;
        function setName($name)
        {
                $this->name = $name;
        }

        function getName()
        {
                return $this->name;
        }
}

class Laptop extends Item
{
        var $price;
        function setPrice($price)
        {
                $this->price = $price;
        }

        function getPrice()
        {
                return $this->price;
        }
}
```

```
$laptop1 = new Laptop;

$laptop1->setName("Sonny Laptop");
$laptop1->setPrice(450);

echo $laptop1->getName().'<br>';
echo $laptop1->getPrice();

?>

</body>

</html>
```

In Example 1, we have created a parent class named Item which contains one variable, $name, and two methods to set and get the name of the item. Next, we created another class, Laptop, which inherits the Item class. To inherit from a class, the "extends" keyword is used.

If you look at the declaration of the Laptop class, you can see it extends Item. Finally, we created an object in the Laptop class and called the setName method. Though the Laptop class doesn't contain any setName method but rather is inheriting the Item class that contains this method, the setName method is available to the child class as well. This is how inheritance work. The output of Example 1 is as follows:

```
Sonny Laptop
450
```

Function Overriding

If both the parent and child classes have methods with the same name and signature, the child class overrides the method in the parent class; this means that if you call the method from the child class now, the method that exists in the child class will be executed rather than the method with same name in the parent class. The following example demonstrates this.

Example 2:

```
<!DOCTYPE html>
<html>
<head>
<title>Chapter 9</title>
</head>

<body>

<?php

class Item
{
        var $name;
        function setName($name)
        {
                $this->name = $name;
        }
```

```
        function getName()
        {
                return $this->name;
        }
}

class Laptop extends Item
{
        var $price;
        function setPrice($price)
        {
                $this->price = $price;
        }

        function getPrice()
        {
                return $this->price;
        }

        function getName()
        {
                return "this is a child function";
        }
}

$laptop1 = new Laptop;

$laptop1->setName("Sonny Laptop");
$laptop1->setPrice(450);

echo $laptop1->getName().'<br>';
echo $laptop1->getPrice();

?>
```

```
</body>

</html>
```

In Example 2, we added a method called getName in the child Laptop class as well. Now, both the Item and Laptop classes have this method. If you call this method from the child class, it will override the parent class getName method and the child class getName method will be executed instead. In the output, the value returned by the child class getName method will be returned. This is shown below:

```
this is a child function
450
```

Calling Parent Class Constructors

Constructors can be called in both the parent class as well as the child class. A question here arises that, when the child class constructor is called to initialize members of the child class, how can the parent class constructor be called from child. The answer is simple. PHP provides a way to call parent class constructors from child classes. The following example demonstrates this concept.

Example 3:

```
<!DOCTYPE html>
<html>
<head>
<title>Chapter 9</title>
</head>

<body>

<?php

class Item
{
        var $name;
        function setName($name)
        {
                $this->name = $name;
        }

        function getName()
        {
                return $this->name;
        }
}

class Laptop extends Item
{
        var $price;
        function __construct($name, $price)
        {
                Item::setName($name);
                $this->price = $price;
        }

        function getPrice()
        {
                return $this->price;
```

```
    }

}

$laptop1 = new Laptop("Sonny", 120);


echo $laptop1->getName().'<br>';
echo $laptop1->getPrice();

?>

</body>

</html>
```

The best way to initialize parent class members is by declaring a method that initializes those members, then call that method in the constructor of the child class passing parameters from the child class. For instance, in Example 3, we have created a constructor inside the Laptop class which accepts two parameters: $name and $price. Inside the constructor, the setName method of the parent Item class has been called using Item::setName($name). This is how we pass the parameter from the child class constructor to a method in the parent class. Finally we have printed the name and price of the Item via the getName and getPrice methods, respectively.

Static Members

The members of a class declared as static can be called and used without instantiating the object of the class. Normal member variables are per instance while static variables are per class. To declare a variable as static, you simply have to add the keyword "static" before the variable name. This is shown in the following example.

Example 4:

```
<!DOCTYPE html>
<html>
<head>
<title>Chapter 9</title>
</head>

<body>

<?php

class Item
{
        var $name;
        public static $price;
        function setName($name)
        {
                $this->name = $name;
        }

        function getName()
        {
                return $this->name;
        }
}

$item1 = new Item;
$item1->setName("Cell Phone");
Item::$price = 500;

echo $item1->getName().'<br>';
```

```
echo Item::$price;

?>

</body>

</html>
```

In the above example, the $price variable has been declared static. You can see that it has been accessed using the class name instead of the variable name.

Exercise 9

Task:

Explain the relationship between the Shape class and Circle class via inheritance. Add appropriate members and methods to demonstrate inheritance. Use constructors to initialize members in both the child and parent classes.

Solution

```
<!DOCTYPE html>
<html>
<head>
<title>Exercise 9</title>
</head>

<body>

<?php
```

```
class Shape
{
        var $name;
        function setProperties($name)
        {
                $this->name = $name;
        }

        function getName()
        {
                return $this->name;
        }
}

class Square extends Shape
{
        var $width, $height;

        function __construct($name, $width, $height)
        {
                Shape::setProperties($name);
                $this->width =$width;
                $this->height = $height;
        }
        function getWidth()
        {
                return $this->width;
        }
        function getHeight()
        {
                return $this->height;
        }
}

$square = new Square("Square Shape", 40, 30);
echo $square->getName().'<br>';
```

```
echo $square->getHeight().'<br>';
echo $square->getWidth();

?>

</body>

</html>
```

Chapter 10: Understanding GET and POST Methods

In the last nine chapters, we have covered most of the core PHP concepts. We have also studied the basics of object oriented programming (OOP) in PHP. We also saw how a PHP engine parses PHP code and returns corresponding HTML. In this chapter, we will learn how to interact with the PHP server from our browser by sending data to the server. We will study basic techniques of sending data to the server and parsing the received data at the server side.

To send data to the PHP server, there are two methods that can be used in the form's action "method" attribute. They are as follows:

- GET Method
- POST Method

We shall see working examples of both of these methods later; first, let's look at the concept of URL encoding.

URL Encoding

When a browser sends information to the server, it appends the information at the end of the URL based on the request being made. This URL is known as a query string and the format of this query string is called URL encoding. Typically, a query string consists of name-value pairs and has the following format:

www.somerandomwebsite.com/index.html?pname=apple&ppric e=250&pcat=fruits

In the above URL, if you look at the end of index.html you will find a "?"; this marks the beginning of the parameters to be passed in the string. Next, we have passed three name-value pairs, each separated by an ampersand symbol. When the request for the above URL is received by the PHP server, it looks for the parameters passed in the URL and performs the appropriate action against it.

1- **GET Method**

Using the GET method, the data passed to the server is encoded in the query string, as explained above. For a better understanding of this concept, have a look at the following example.

Example 1:

Create an HTML page with following content.

```
<!DOCTYPE html>
<html>
```

```
<head>
<title>Chapter 10</title>
</head>

<body>

<form action="http://localhost/test.php"
method="get">
<input type="text" name="pname" placeholder="Product
Name"></input><br/>
<input type="text" name="pprice" placeholder="Product
Price"></input><br/>
<input type="text" name="pcat" placeholder="Product
Category"></input><br/>
<input type="submit" name="submit"
value="Submit"></input>
</form>


</body>

</html>
```

In Example 1, we created a form and, in its action attribute, we passed a URL of a PHP page. Next, we passed "get" in the method attribute of the form. This means that, when this form is submitted, the data of the form will be passed to the URL specified in the action attribute, which in our case is test.php, located at localhost.

Create a test.php file and place it in the "www" directory. The content of test.php should look like this:

```
<!DOCTYPE html>
```

```
<html>
<head>
<title>Chapter 10</title>
</head>

<body>

<h1>This is posted via get method</h1>
<?php
if( $_GET["pname"] || $_GET["pprice"] ||
$_GET["pcat"])
{
echo "Product Name: ". $_GET['pname']. "<br />";
echo "Product Price: ". $_GET["pprice"]. "<br />";
echo "Product Category: ". $_GET["pcat"];
}
?>

</body>

</html>
```

In test.php, we have to get the content of the query string that was passed with the URL when the submit button was clicked on the HTML page created in the previous code snippet. To retrieve the content of the query string, the $_GET associative array is used and the name of the parameter whose value has to be accessed is passed as the index. For example, if you want to get the value of the pname parameter, just pass it in the form of a string as index to the $_GET associative array. Using this technique, the value of pname, pprice, and pcat have been displayed on the test.php page.

Now, if you enter some data in the form on the first page and click the button, you will be redirected to the test.php. This is shown in the following two snapshots:

Apple
250
Fruits
Submit

Clicking the submit button will redirect you to the following page:

This is posted via get method

Product Name: Apple
Product Price: 250
Product Category: Fruits

If you look at the URL in the address bar, you can see that form data has been encoded in the URL in query string format. This is how the GET method works.

Since the GET method encodes form information in the query string, never use the GET method to send sensitive information, such as passwords, to the server. Furthermore, the GET method cannot be used to send images and other binary data to the server.

2- Post Method

The POST method can also be used to send information to the server. The POST method doesn't include information in the query string; rather, the information is passed via HTTP header. Therefore, security is defined by HTTP protocol. Let's modify Example 1 to post data to test.php via the POST method and then display it on test.php.

Example 2:

Change the form in Example 1 as follows:

```
<form action="http://localhost/test.php"
method="post">
<input type="text" name="pname" placeholder="Product
Name"></input><br/>
<input type="text" name="pprice" placeholder="Product
Price"></input><br/>
<input type="text" name="pcat" placeholder="Product
Category"></input><br/>
<input type="submit" name="submit"
value="Submit"></input>
</form>
```

You can see that the method attribute of the form has been changed to "post". Now, modify the test.php page as follows:

```
<!DOCTYPE html>
<html>
<head>
<title>Chapter 10</title>
</head>

<body>
```

```
<h1>This is posted via POST method</h1>
<?php
if(    $_POST["pname"]    ||    $_POST["pprice"]    ||
$_POST["pcat"])
{
echo "Product Name: ". $_POST['pname']. "<br />";
echo "Product Price: ". $_POST["pprice"]. "<br />";
echo "Product Category: ". $_POST["pcat"];
}
?>
</body>

</html>
```

Now, if you enter some data in the form and press the submit button, you will see the following page:

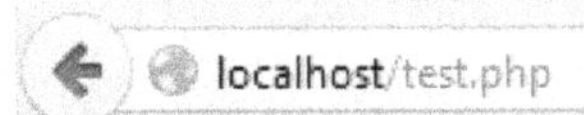

You can see that the URL no longer contains any form data. Hence, POST is a more secure and robust way of interacting with the server.

Exercise 10

Task:

Create a form with two fields: name and salary. Pass this data to the server via the POST method. Calculate a 10% bonus on the salary and display Name, Salary, and Bonus on the salary.php page.

Solution

Form Page

```
<!DOCTYPE html>
<html>
<head>
<title>Exercise 10</title>
</head>

<body>

<form action="http://localhost/salary.php"
method="post">
<input type="text" name="name"
placeholder="Name"></input><br/>
<input type="text" name="salary"
placeholder="Salary"></input><br/>
<input type="submit" name="submit"
value="Submit"></input>
</form>


</body>

</html>
```

salary.php

```
<!DOCTYPE html>
<html>
<head>
<title>Exercise 10</title>
</head>

<body>

<?php
if( $_POST["name"] || $_POST["salary"])
{
echo "Name: ". $_POST['name']. "<br />";
echo "Salary: ". $_POST['salary']. "<br />";

$bonus = $_POST["salary"]/10;
echo "Bonus on Salary: ". $bonus;
}
?>
</body>

</html>
```

Other Books by the Author

C# Programming for Beginners
http://www.linuxtrainingacademy.com/c-sharp

C# is a simple and general-purpose object-oriented programming language. Combine this with its versatility and huge standard library it's easy to see why it's such a popular and well-respected programming language.

When you learn how to program in C# you will be able to develop web based applications or graphical desktop applications. One of the best things about C# is that it's easy to learn... especially with this book.

Java Programming
http://www.linuxtrainingacademy.com/java-programming

Java is one of the most widely used and powerful computer programming languages in existence today. Once you learn how to program in Java you can create software applications that run on servers, desktop computers, tablets, phones, Blu-ray players, and more.

Also, if you want to ensure your software behaves the same regardless of which operation system it runs on, then Java's "write once, run anywhere" philosophy is for you. Java was design to be platform independent allowing you to create applications that run on a variety of operating systems including Windows, Mac, Solaris, and Linux.

JavaScript: A Guide to Learning the JavaScript Programming Language
http://www.linuxtrainingacademy.com/javascript

JavaScript is a dynamic computer programming language that is commonly used in web browsers to control the behavior of web pages and interact with users. It allows for asynchronous communication and can update parts of a web page or even replace the entire content of a web page. You'll see JavaScript being used to display date and time information, perform animations on a web site, validate form input, suggest results as a user types into a search box, and more.

Scrum Essentials: Agile Software Development and Agile Project Management for Project Managers, Scrum Masters, Product Owners, and Stakeholders
http://www.linuxtrainingacademy.com/scrum-book

You have a limited amount of time to create software, especially when you're given a deadline, self-imposed or not. You'll want to make sure that the software you build is at least decent but more importantly, on time. How do you balance quality with time? This book dives into these very important topics and more.

Additional Resources

Learn PHP Programming from Scratch Course
http://www.linuxtrainingacademy.com/php-from-scratch

This is a comprehensive PHP course. You will learn everything from the basics to more advanced PHP programming techniques using real world examples and sample projects.

CPSIA information can be obtained
at www.ICGtesting.com
Printed in the USA
LVHW012126210519
618618LV00017B/1277/P

9 781511 594226